This Pet Journal Belongs To:

MY PET *Profile*

NAME:

BREED:

BIRTHDAY:

GENDER:

ID CHIP #:

ALLERGIES:

COAT COLOR:

EYE COLOR:

SPECIAL MARKINGS:

MEDICAL CONDITIONS:

WEIGHT :

FAVORITE TOYS:

SPAY/NEUTERED: YES: NO:

NOTES:

Vet Information

NAME/BUSINESS:

PHONE:

EMAIL:

ADDRESS:

Groomer Information

NAME/BUSINESS:

PHONE:

EMAIL:

ADDRESS:

PET *Vaccination Chart*

YEAR:

PET NAME: **DOB:**   **GENDER:**

VACCINATION HISTORY

DATE:	VACCINATION:	AGE:	NOTES:

VETERINARY CARE *Tracker*

DATE:	DESCRIPTION:	LOCATION:	AMOUNT:

PET HEALTH
Immunization Records

DATE:	AGE:	TYPE:	GIVEN BY:	NEXT DUE:

PET HEALTH
Medication Records

DATE:	AGE:	MEDICATION:	GIVEN BY:	NEXT DUE:

PET MEDICATION *Tracker*

DATE & TIME:	MEDICATION:	FREQUENCY:	DOSAGE:

PET WELLNESS *Journal*

YEAR:

PET NAME: DOB: GENDER:

WELLNESS HISTORY

DATE:	DESCRIPTION:	TREATMENT:	NOTES:

PET SITTER *Notes*
- RESPONSIBILITIES -

	M	T	W	T	F	S	S

MY PET Expenses

MONTH:　　　　　　　　　　　　　**YEAR:**

PET NAME:

EXPENSE TRACKER

DATE	FOOD	VET	MEDICATION	GROOMING	COST
					$
					$
					$
					$
					$
					$
					$
					$
					$
					$
					$
					$
					$
					$
					$

MY PET Expenses

MONTH: **YEAR:**

PET NAME:

EXPENSE TRACKER

DATE	FOOD	VET	MEDICATION	GROOMING	COST
					$
					$
					$
					$
					$
					$
					$
					$
					$
					$
					$
					$
					$
					$
					$
					$
					$

MONTHLY PET *Overview*

JANUARY

FEBRUARY

MARCH

APRIL

MAY

JUNE

MONTHLY PET *Overview*

JULY	AUGUST	SEPTEMBER

OCTOBER	NOVEMBER	DECEMBER

WEEKLY PET *Journal*

WEEK OF: _____

MONDAY	TUESDAY	WEDNESDAY

THURSDAY	FRIDAY	SATURDAY

SUNDAY

WEEKLY NOTES

MY PET Journal

WEEKLY PET *Journal*

WEEK OF: _____

MONDAY   **TUESDAY**   **WEDNESDAY**

THURSDAY   **FRIDAY**   **SATURDAY**

SUNDAY   **WEEKLY NOTES**

MY PET Journal

_____

_____

_____

_____

_____

_____

_____

_____

_____

_____

_____

_____

_____

_____

_____

_____

_____

WEEKLY PET *Journal*

WEEK OF: _____

MONDAY	TUESDAY	WEDNESDAY

THURSDAY	FRIDAY	SATURDAY

SUNDAY	WEEKLY NOTES

MY PET Journal

_____
_____
_____
_____
_____
_____
_____
_____
_____
_____
_____
_____
_____
_____
_____
_____
_____
_____
_____

WEEKLY PET *Journal*

WEEK OF: _____

MONDAY	TUESDAY	WEDNESDAY

THURSDAY	FRIDAY	SATURDAY

SUNDAY	WEEKLY NOTES

MY PET Journal

WEEKLY PET *Journal*

MONDAY

TUESDAY

WEDNESDAY

THURSDAY

FRIDAY

SATURDAY

SUNDAY

WEEKLY NOTES

MY PET *Journal*

_____
_____
_____
_____
_____
_____
_____
_____
_____
_____
_____
_____
_____
_____
_____
_____
_____
_____
_____
_____

WEEKLY PET *Journal*

MONDAY

TUESDAY

WEDNESDAY

THURSDAY

FRIDAY

SATURDAY

SUNDAY

WEEKLY NOTES

MY PET Journal

WEEKLY PET *Journal*

MONDAY

TUESDAY

WEDNESDAY

THURSDAY

FRIDAY

SATURDAY

SUNDAY

WEEKLY NOTES

MY PET Journal

WEEKLY PET *Journal*

WEEK OF: _____

MONDAY   **TUESDAY**   **WEDNESDAY**

THURSDAY   **FRIDAY**   **SATURDAY**

SUNDAY   **WEEKLY NOTES**

MY PET Journal

_____

_____

_____

_____

_____

_____

_____

_____

_____

_____

_____

_____

_____

_____

_____

_____

_____

_____

WEEKLY PET *Journal*

MONDAY   **TUESDAY**   **WEDNESDAY**

THURSDAY   **FRIDAY**   **SATURDAY**

SUNDAY   **WEEKLY NOTES**

MY PET Journal

_____

_____

_____

_____

_____

_____

_____

_____

_____

_____

_____

_____

_____

_____

_____

_____

_____

_____

WEEKLY PET *Journal*

MONDAY

TUESDAY

WEDNESDAY

THURSDAY

FRIDAY

SATURDAY

SUNDAY

WEEKLY NOTES

MY PET Journal

WEEKLY PET *Journal*

WEEK OF: _____

MONDAY

TUESDAY

WEDNESDAY

THURSDAY

FRIDAY

SATURDAY

SUNDAY

WEEKLY NOTES

MY PET Journal

WEEKLY PET *Journal*

WEEK OF: _____

MONDAY	TUESDAY	WEDNESDAY

THURSDAY	FRIDAY	SATURDAY

SUNDAY

WEEKLY NOTES

MY PET Journal

_____

_____

_____

_____

_____

_____

_____

_____

_____

_____

_____

_____

_____

_____

_____

_____

_____

_____

_____

WEEKLY PET *Journal*

WEEK OF: _____

MONDAY	TUESDAY	WEDNESDAY

THURSDAY	FRIDAY	SATURDAY

SUNDAY

WEEKLY NOTES

MY PET Journal

_____
_____
_____
_____
_____
_____
_____
_____
_____
_____
_____
_____
_____
_____
_____
_____

WEEKLY PET *Journal*

WEEK OF: _____

MONDAY   **TUESDAY**   **WEDNESDAY**

THURSDAY   **FRIDAY**   **SATURDAY**

SUNDAY   **WEEKLY NOTES**

MY PET Journal

WEEKLY PET *Journal*

WEEK OF: _____

MONDAY

TUESDAY

WEDNESDAY

THURSDAY

FRIDAY

SATURDAY

SUNDAY

WEEKLY NOTES

MY PET Journal

_____

_____

_____

_____

_____

_____

_____

_____

_____

_____

_____

_____

_____

_____

_____

_____

_____

_____

WEEKLY PET *Journal*

WEEK OF: _____

MONDAY	TUESDAY	WEDNESDAY

THURSDAY	FRIDAY	SATURDAY

SUNDAY	WEEKLY NOTES

MY PET Journal

_____
_____
_____
_____
_____
_____
_____
_____
_____
_____
_____
_____
_____
_____
_____
_____
_____
_____
_____

WEEKLY PET *Journal*

WEEK OF: _____

MONDAY

TUESDAY

WEDNESDAY

THURSDAY

FRIDAY

SATURDAY

SUNDAY

WEEKLY NOTES

MY PET Journal

WEEKLY PET *Journal*

WEEK OF: _____

MONDAY

TUESDAY

WEDNESDAY

THURSDAY

FRIDAY

SATURDAY

SUNDAY

WEEKLY NOTES

MY PET Journal

_____

_____

_____

_____

_____

_____

_____

_____

_____

_____

_____

_____

_____

_____

_____

_____

_____

WEEKLY PET *Journal*

WEEK OF: _____

MONDAY	TUESDAY	WEDNESDAY

THURSDAY	FRIDAY	SATURDAY

SUNDAY	WEEKLY NOTES

MY PET Journal

_____
_____
_____
_____
_____
_____
_____
_____
_____
_____
_____
_____
_____
_____
_____
_____
_____
_____
_____

WEEKLY PET *Journal*

WEEK OF: _____

MONDAY

TUESDAY

WEDNESDAY

THURSDAY

FRIDAY

SATURDAY

SUNDAY

WEEKLY NOTES

MY PET Journal

WEEKLY PET *Journal*

WEEK OF: _____

MONDAY	TUESDAY	WEDNESDAY

THURSDAY	FRIDAY	SATURDAY

SUNDAY

WEEKLY NOTES

MY PET Journal

WEEKLY PET *Journal*

MONDAY

TUESDAY

WEDNESDAY

THURSDAY

FRIDAY

SATURDAY

SUNDAY

WEEKLY NOTES

MY PET Journal

WEEKLY PET *Journal*

WEEK OF: _____

MONDAY

TUESDAY

WEDNESDAY

THURSDAY

FRIDAY

SATURDAY

SUNDAY

WEEKLY NOTES

MY PET Journal

_____
_____
_____
_____
_____
_____
_____
_____
_____
_____
_____
_____
_____
_____
_____
_____
_____
_____

WEEKLY PET *Journal*

WEEK OF: _____

MONDAY   **TUESDAY**   **WEDNESDAY**

THURSDAY   **FRIDAY**   **SATURDAY**

SUNDAY   **WEEKLY NOTES**

MY PET Journal

WEEKLY PET *Journal*

WEEK OF: _____

MONDAY	TUESDAY	WEDNESDAY

THURSDAY	FRIDAY	SATURDAY

SUNDAY	WEEKLY NOTES

MY PET Journal

WEEKLY PET *Journal*

WEEK OF: _____

MONDAY	TUESDAY	WEDNESDAY

THURSDAY	FRIDAY	SATURDAY

SUNDAY	WEEKLY NOTES

MY PET Journal

_____

_____

_____

_____

_____

_____

_____

_____

_____

_____

_____

_____

_____

_____

_____

_____

WEEKLY PET *Journal*

_____

MONDAY

TUESDAY

WEDNESDAY

THURSDAY

FRIDAY

SATURDAY

SUNDAY

WEEKLY NOTES

MY PET Journal

WEEKLY PET *Journal*

WEEK OF: _____

MONDAY

TUESDAY

WEDNESDAY

THURSDAY

FRIDAY

SATURDAY

SUNDAY

WEEKLY NOTES

MY PET Journal

WEEKLY PET *Journal*

WEEK OF: _____

MONDAY	TUESDAY	WEDNESDAY

THURSDAY	FRIDAY	SATURDAY

SUNDAY	WEEKLY NOTES

MY PET Journal

WEEKLY PET *Journal*

WEEK OF: _____

MONDAY

TUESDAY

WEDNESDAY

THURSDAY

FRIDAY

SATURDAY

SUNDAY

WEEKLY NOTES

MY PET Journal

WEEKLY PET *Journal*

MONDAY	TUESDAY	WEDNESDAY

THURSDAY	FRIDAY	SATURDAY

SUNDAY

WEEKLY NOTES

MY PET Journal

_____
_____
_____
_____
_____
_____
_____
_____
_____
_____
_____
_____
_____
_____
_____
_____
_____
_____

WEEKLY PET *Journal*

WEEK OF: _____

MONDAY

TUESDAY

WEDNESDAY

THURSDAY

FRIDAY

SATURDAY

SUNDAY

WEEKLY NOTES

MY PET Journal

WEEKLY PET *Journal*

WEEK OF: _____

MONDAY	TUESDAY	WEDNESDAY

THURSDAY	FRIDAY	SATURDAY

SUNDAY	WEEKLY NOTES

MY PET Journal

_____
_____
_____
_____
_____
_____
_____
_____
_____
_____
_____
_____
_____
_____
_____
_____
_____
_____

WEEKLY PET *Journal*

MONDAY

TUESDAY

WEDNESDAY

THURSDAY

FRIDAY

SATURDAY

SUNDAY

WEEKLY NOTES

MY PET Journal

_____
_____
_____
_____
_____
_____
_____
_____
_____
_____
_____
_____
_____
_____
_____
_____
_____
_____
_____
_____

WEEKLY PET *Journal*

MONDAY

TUESDAY

WEDNESDAY

THURSDAY

FRIDAY

SATURDAY

SUNDAY

WEEKLY NOTES

MY PET Journal

WEEKLY PET *Journal*

WEEK OF: ....

MONDAY	TUESDAY	WEDNESDAY

THURSDAY	FRIDAY	SATURDAY

SUNDAY	WEEKLY NOTES

MY PET Journal

_____
_____
_____
_____
_____
_____
_____
_____
_____
_____
_____
_____
_____
_____
_____
_____
_____
_____

WEEKLY PET *Journal*

WEEK OF: _____

MONDAY	TUESDAY	WEDNESDAY

THURSDAY	FRIDAY	SATURDAY

SUNDAY	WEEKLY NOTES

MY PET Journal

WEEKLY PET *Journal*

WEEK OF: ....

MONDAY	TUESDAY	WEDNESDAY

THURSDAY	FRIDAY	SATURDAY

SUNDAY

WEEKLY NOTES

MY PET Journal

_____
_____
_____
_____
_____
_____
_____
_____
_____
_____
_____
_____
_____
_____
_____
_____
_____
_____
_____

WEEKLY PET *Journal*

WEEK OF: _____

MONDAY	TUESDAY	WEDNESDAY

THURSDAY	FRIDAY	SATURDAY

SUNDAY	WEEKLY NOTES

MY PET Journal

WEEKLY PET *Journal*

WEEK OF: _____

MONDAY	TUESDAY	WEDNESDAY

THURSDAY	FRIDAY	SATURDAY

SUNDAY

WEEKLY NOTES

MY PET Journal

WEEKLY PET *Journal*

WEEK OF: _____

MONDAY

TUESDAY

WEDNESDAY

THURSDAY

FRIDAY

SATURDAY

SUNDAY

WEEKLY NOTES

MY PET Journal

WEEKLY PET *Journal*

WEEK OF: _____

MONDAY	TUESDAY	WEDNESDAY

THURSDAY	FRIDAY	SATURDAY

SUNDAY	WEEKLY NOTES

MY PET Journal

_____
_____
_____
_____
_____
_____
_____
_____
_____
_____
_____
_____
_____
_____
_____
_____
_____

WEEKLY PET *Journal*

WEEK OF: _____

MONDAY

TUESDAY

WEDNESDAY

THURSDAY

FRIDAY

SATURDAY

SUNDAY

WEEKLY NOTES

MY PET *Journal*

WEEKLY PET *Journal*

WEEK OF: _____

MONDAY

TUESDAY

WEDNESDAY

THURSDAY

FRIDAY

SATURDAY

SUNDAY

WEEKLY NOTES

MY PET Journal

WEEKLY PET *Journal*

WEEK OF: _____

MONDAY

TUESDAY

WEDNESDAY

THURSDAY

FRIDAY

SATURDAY

SUNDAY

WEEKLY NOTES

MY PET Journal

_____

_____

_____

_____

_____

_____

_____

_____

_____

_____

_____

_____

_____

_____

_____

WEEKLY PET *Journal*

WEEK OF: _____

MONDAY

TUESDAY

WEDNESDAY

THURSDAY

FRIDAY

SATURDAY

SUNDAY

WEEKLY NOTES

MY PET Journal

WEEKLY PET *Journal*

WEEK OF: _____

MONDAY   **TUESDAY**   **WEDNESDAY**

THURSDAY   **FRIDAY**   **SATURDAY**

SUNDAY   **WEEKLY NOTES**

MY PET Journal

_____

_____

_____

_____

_____

_____

_____

_____

_____

_____

_____

_____

_____

_____

_____

_____

_____

_____

_____

_____

WEEKLY PET *Journal*

WEEK OF: _____

MONDAY

TUESDAY

WEDNESDAY

THURSDAY

FRIDAY

SATURDAY

SUNDAY

WEEKLY NOTES

MY PET Journal

WEEKLY PET *Journal*

WEEK OF: _____

MONDAY   TUESDAY   WEDNESDAY

THURSDAY   FRIDAY   SATURDAY

SUNDAY   WEEKLY NOTES

MY PET Journal

_____
_____
_____
_____
_____
_____
_____
_____
_____
_____
_____
_____
_____
_____
_____
_____
_____
_____
_____
_____
_____
_____
_____

WEEKLY PET *Journal*

WEEK OF: _____

MONDAY	TUESDAY	WEDNESDAY

THURSDAY	FRIDAY	SATURDAY

SUNDAY	WEEKLY NOTES

MY PET Journal

WEEKLY PET *Journal*

MONDAY

TUESDAY

WEDNESDAY

THURSDAY

FRIDAY

SATURDAY

SUNDAY

WEEKLY NOTES

MY PET Journal

_____
_____
_____
_____
_____
_____
_____
_____
_____
_____
_____
_____
_____
_____
_____
_____
_____
_____
_____

WEEKLY PET *Journal*

MONDAY

TUESDAY

WEDNESDAY

THURSDAY

FRIDAY

SATURDAY

SUNDAY

WEEKLY NOTES

MY PET Journal

_____

_____

_____

_____

_____

_____

_____

_____

_____

_____

_____

_____

_____

_____

_____

_____

_____

_____

MY PET Journal

MY PET Journal

Made in the USA
Las Vegas, NV
15 August 2021